JACOB DOWDELL JR.
CO-AUTHOR, **KATRINA MONTEZ DOWDELL**

BIG JAKE'S STROKE OF GENIUS

THE ROAD TO 120/80

A STEP-BY-STEP GUIDE TO TRANSFORMING YOUR STROKE
RECOVERY INTO A JOURNEY OF STRENGTH AND HOPE

AMARO GROUP
PUBLISHING

Mt Pleasant, SC
www.AmaroGroupServices.com
Big Jake's Stroke of Genius: The Road to 20/180
©2025 Jacob Dowdell Jr.

ALL RIGHTS RESERVED

No portion of this book may be reproduced, stored in a retrieval system, or transmitted in any form by electronic, mechanical, photocopy, recording, or other–except for brief quotations in printed reviews without prior permission of the author.

Paperback: 978-1-961673-08-3

TABLE OF CONTENTS

01 UNDERSTANDING THE BATTLEFIELD
The Science of Stroke — **13**

02 MAPPING THE TERRAIN
Navigating Recovery — **23**

03 STRENGTHENING THE MIND
Cognitive and Emotional Healing — **39**

04 THE SUPPORT SQUAD
Building a Strong Network — **47**

05 A NEW MISSION
Living Beyond Recovery — **53**

06 THE 21-DAY WELLNESS JOURNEY
Blood Pressure Logs — **67**

INTRODUCTION

Life can change in an instant. One moment, I was living my life to the fullest coaching, running, and embracing every challenge with a warrior spirit. The next, I found myself waking up in a hospital bed, grappling with the aftermath of multiple strokes and the new reality of living with Epilepsy. In that moment of vulnerability, I realized that my journey was not just about survival; it was about transformation. "Big Jake's Stroke of Genius: The Road to 120/180" is a testament to resilience, hope, and the power of community. This book chronicles my personal journey through the trials of recovery, not only from strokes but also from the emotional and cognitive challenges that accompany them. It serves as a guide for stroke survivors, caregivers, and anyone navigating their own battles.

Throughout these pages, you will find insights drawn from my experiences, supported by the love and strength of those around me—my fiancée at the time, Katrina (now my wife), friends, coaches, and a network of incredible individuals who rallied to lift me up when I needed it most.

Together, we built a community that transformed adversity into opportunity.

Each chapter delves into crucial aspects of recovery, from understanding the science of strokes to developing mental resilience, building a support network, and discovering new missions in life. You will find practical exercises, heartfelt anecdotes, and actionable steps to empower your own journey toward recovery and well-being.

BEFORE YOU BEGIN

As you embark on this journey, it's essential to assess where you currently stand in your recovery process. This assessment will help you reflect on your support systems, coping mechanisms, and readiness to engage in the transformative work that lies ahead.

BIG JAKE'S STROKE OF GENIUS 8

RECOVERY READINESS ASSESSMENT

Instructions: For each statement below, read carefully and assign points based on your current feelings or situations.

1 = NOT AT ALL TRUE   2 = RARELY TRUE   3 = SOMETIMES TRUE
4 = OFTEN TRUE   5 = VERY TRUE

QUESTION	RATING/POINTS				
I feel I have a solid understanding of what a stroke is and its potential impacts.	1	2	3	4	5
I have a support system (friends, family, community) that I can rely on during my recovery.	1	2	3	4	5
I actively seek information and resources about recovery and health improvement.	1	2	3	4	5
I have set specific, measurable goals for my recovery process.	1	2	3	4	5
I regularly engage in physical activities that promote my health and well-being.	1	2	3	4	5
I take time to reflect on my achievements and celebrate my progress, no matter how small.	1	2	3	4	5
I practice mindfulness or relaxation techniques to manage stress and emotions.	1	2	3	4	5
I maintain a positive outlook and believe in my ability to recover and improve my quality of life.	1	2	3	4	5
I communicate openly with my healthcare providers about my needs and concerns.	1	2	3	4	5
I actively participate in support groups or communities related to stroke recovery or health improvement.	1	2	3	4	5

WHAT YOUR RECOVERY READINESS ASSESSMENT SCORE MEANS

10-20 Points: Just Getting Started
You may be at the beginning of your recovery journey or feeling overwhelmed. It's important to take small steps and seek support to help you understand your situation better. Consider connecting with resources and support groups to empower your journey.

21-30 Points: On the Right Track
You have some understanding and support in place, but there may be areas where you can improve. Focus on setting specific goals and engaging more with your community to enhance your recovery process.

31-50 Points: Ready for Action
You are well-prepared and motivated to take charge of your recovery. Keep building on your strengths, maintaining your positive mindset, and supporting others in their journeys. Your experience and insights can inspire those around you.

Recovery is a journey filled with ups and downs but remember that you are not alone. Building a supportive network and embracing the challenges ahead can lead to profound transformations. The insights, stories, and strategies shared in this book are designed to guide you through the complexities of recovery, helping you discover new strengths and possibilities.

As we move forward, I encourage you to approach each chapter with an open heart and mind. Celebrate your victories, no matter how small, and acknowledge the courage it takes to confront each day.

CAREGIVER ASSESSMENT

For caregivers supporting stroke survivors, this assessment helps gauge your current state of readiness and ability to provide effective support.

**1 = NOT AT ALL TRUE   2 = RARELY TRUE   3 = SOMETIMES TRUE
4 = OFTEN TRUE   5 = VERY TRUE**

QUESTION	RATING/POINTS
I feel knowledgeable about stroke recovery processes and what the survivor may experience.	1 2 3 4 5
I am open to joining support groups for caregivers.	1 2 3 4 5
I regularly communicate with the stroke survivor about their needs and feelings.	1 2 3 4 5
I practice self-care to ensure I can provide the best support possible.	1 2 3 4 5
I am proactive in seeking resources and information to help in the recovery process.	1 2 3 4 5
I maintain a positive outlook and believe in the survivor's ability to recover.	1 2 3 4 5
I take time to celebrate the small victories of the stroke survivor.	1 2 3 4 5
I have developed coping strategies to manage stress and emotional challenges.	1 2 3 4 5
I actively participate in the survivor's recovery journey and encourage their independence.	1 2 3 4 5
I have a support system (friends, family, other caregivers) to help me cope with my responsibilities.	1 2 3 4 5

WHAT YOUR CAREGIVER ASSESSMENT SCORE MEANS

10-20 Points: Just Getting Started
You may feel overwhelmed by the responsibilities of caregiving. It's crucial to seek support for yourself and understand the resources available to help you in this journey.

21-30 Points: On the Right Track
You have a good understanding of your role, but there may be areas for growth. Consider focusing on your self-care and seeking out additional resources and support groups for caregivers.

31-50 Points: Ready for Action
You are well-prepared and motivated to take charge of your recovery. Keep building on your strengths, maintaining your positive mindset, and supporting others in their journeys. Your experience and insights can inspire those around you.

Welcome to "**Big Jake's Stroke of Genius**": The Road to 20/180." Together, let's turn our challenges into steppingstones, embrace our journeys, and uncover the genius within us all. Your transformation begins now.

CHAPTER ONE
UNDERSTANDING THE BATTLEFIELD
THE SCIENCE OF STROKE

BIG JAKE'S STROKE OF GENIUS   14

UNDERSTANDING THE BATTLEFIELD

THE SCIENCE OF STROKE

Her name was Jessie Mae Woodson but to me and all her grandchildren, her name was Ma Jessie. Growing up in the deep south, calling adults by their first name was a punishable offense. Ma Jessie was my first encounter with a stroke. Prior to her stroke, I was a frequent visitor at Ma Jesse's house on Rabbitneck St. She would always feed me double portions. She'd tell me I need to "put meat on my bones" if I wanted to play football for our neighborhood team, the Rabbitneck Cowboys. I was known as the runt in the family, but I was her favorite grandchild.

I was around eight or nine years old when she had the stroke and moved in with us. A hospital bed was placed in the middle bedroom for her. I suffered from insomnia as a kid, so I became her around the clock caretaker and roommate. I never found out why I didn't require much sleep, but it always seemed to work to my advantage. It allowed me to spend more time with Ma Jessie which gave me the opportunity to learn some of the basic Swahili vocabulary. As I recall, she was only able to communicate in Swahili after the stroke. Prior to having the stroke, she would sing in Swahili, but the stroke caused her paralysis and robbed her of her beautiful singing voice. Ma Jessie's grandmother was a sharecropper, and her great grandmother was a slave. Ma Jessie kept an oral history of her upbringing and the language. I was fascinated when she would share stories with me and deeply sadden when she was unable to due to the stroke.

Having to take care of Ma Jessie, who had always taken care of me and given me a safe place to be in her home made me a very empathetic person. Being so young and small I was aware of my physical limitations to help her. The most I could do was pray and ask God to help. I remember telling God I was going to become the world's best at praying so He could heal her. I developed a deep sense of spirituality and faith which would later result in me becoming an ordained minister. As I grew older and experienced strokes myself, I began to understand the true impact of what happened to Ma Jessie. What once seemed like a mysterious and frightening event now became something I could identify and explain. Her experience with stroke, as well as my own, taught me the importance of understanding what a stroke truly is and how it affects the body.

Back then, I didn't know anything about stroke or epilepsy. We just called it a "spell" when she was having an epileptic seizure that was a result of her first stroke. Nurse Helen, Ma Jessie's in home nurse, would say, "120/80 is the most important numbers in your life", when she would take Ma Jessie's blood pressure. At that time, I was just impressed with the stethoscope and the gag on the blood pressure cuff; and the fact she would call me her boyfriend and tell me I was doing such a great job taking care of Ma Jessie. After surviving several strokes myself, I now realized nurse Helen was right about the blood pressure. I've also come to know more about strokes and how it is an interruption of blood flood to the brain. There are two main types of strokes; ischemic and hemorrhagic which are classified based on the cause of the stroke. An ischemic stroke occurs when a blood clot, known as a thrombus, blocks or plugs an artery leading to the brain. A blood clot often forms in arteries damaged by a buildup of plaques, known as atherosclerosis. Atherosclerosis, often referred to as the hardening of the arteries, occurs when fats, cholesterol, and other substances build up on the artery walls. Think of it as a blockage in a pipe that restricts the flow of water—in this case, the flow of blood to vital parts of the brain. This blockage can increase the risk of a blood clot forming, leading to an ischemic stroke. Hemorrhagic stroke is due to bleeding into the brain by the rupture of a blood vessel. Hemorrhagic stroke may be further subdivided into intracerebral hemorrhage (ICH) (An emergency condition in which a ruptured blood vessel causes bleeding inside the brain) and subarachnoid hemorrhage (SAH) (Bleeding in the space between the brain and the tissue covering the brain). Hemorrhagic stroke is associated with severe morbidity and high mortality. According to the World Health Organization (WHO), 15 million people suffer from stroke worldwide each year. Over 41,000 people a day have a stroke. The good news is recovery is possible with early detection coupled with a strong support system. Many people can either fully recover or lessen the effect of the stroke.

There are many causes of stroke. Some risk factors that can lead to stroke are diabetes, high cholesterol, family history, smoking, obesity, and heart disease. However, the leading cause of stroke is unregulated hypertension. This is why it is essential to know your blood pressure numbers while you are on the road to 120/80. The top number is called "systolic blood pressure" (120) and measures blood pressure when the heart pumps. The bottom number is called "diastolic blood pressure" (80) and measures blood pressure when the heart rests between beats. Monitoring these two numbers and making the necessary changes in your lifestyle when they are in a range of hypertension (about 140/90) will decrease the potential strain and damage to the arteries that ultimately lead to stroke. Whether you're reading this because you've experienced a stroke yourself, you're caring for someone who has, or you're simply looking to protect your health, it's natural to feel worried or uncertain. Strokes can be sudden and life-altering, but with the right knowledge and tools, you can take control of your health and reduce the risk. The goal of this book is to do both while giving you the tools to make life changes that will avoid stroke altogether. This chapter, and this book, is here to empower you on that journey.

A key component of surviving a stroke is recognizing the signs as quickly as possible. The faster you can identify the symptoms, the sooner you can receive medical attention, which can make a significant difference in the outcome of recovery.

To help identify the symptoms, there is a widely recognized acronym we use: "FAST". This simple yet powerful tool can aid in identifying a stroke and getting immediate help. By remembering and acting on the FAST acronym, you could be saving someone's life or preserving their quality of life.

> **F** - Facial Drooping: One of the most noticeable signs of a stroke is a drooping or uneven smile. Ask the person to smile and check if one side of the face droops. Facial asymmetry can indicate that part of the brain is not functioning properly, which is often a sign of stroke.
>
> **A** - Arm weakness or numbness is a common stroke symptom. Ask the person to raise both arms. If one arm cannot be raised or is significantly delayed in responding to the command, it may indicate a stroke affecting the brain's motor control area.

S - Speech Difficulty: Speech problems often occur with a stroke. The person may have slurred speech or trouble finding the right words. Ask the person to repeat a simple sentence, and see if they have difficulty speaking or if their words sound unclear. This symptom can indicate that the part of the brain responsible for language is being affected.

T - Time to Call 911: Time is critical when it comes to strokes. The faster the person can be evaluated and treated in a hospital, the better the chances for recovery and minimizing damage. Don't wait, and don't hesitate.

The **FAST** acronym serves as a crucial reminder for everyone to stay alert to the signs of a stroke.

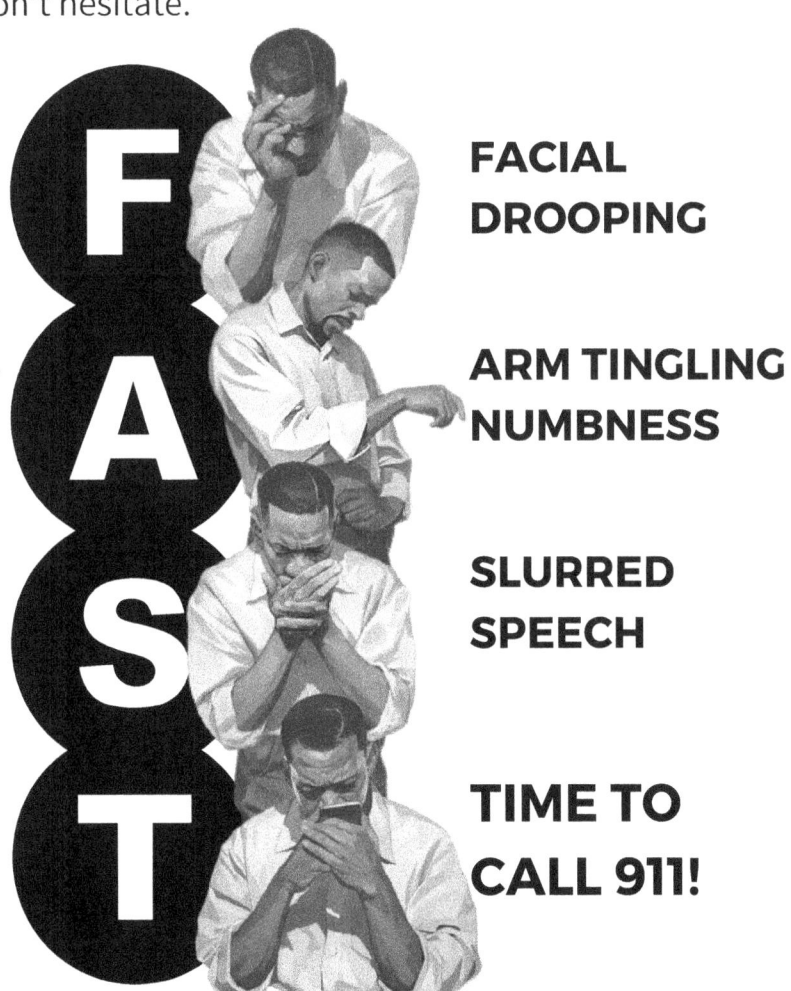

F FACIAL DROOPING

A ARM TINGLING NUMBNESS

S SLURRED SPEECH

T TIME TO CALL 911!

Being an athlete all my life, I never thought that stroke would be something that I had to worry about. I now know all the factors that go into having a stroke and more importantly surviving. It is my goal to help those who have a stroke to not only survive but to thrive with a special emphasis on proper nutrition and mental health. In this chapter, we've explored what a stroke is, the different types of strokes, and the key risk factors to watch out for. By understanding these critical aspects, you're taking the first step toward protecting yourself and your loved ones. Remember, early detection and maintaining healthy blood pressure are your best defenses against stroke. As we move forward in this book, we'll delve deeper into the strategies that can help you not just survive but thrive, even in the face of adversity.

CHAPTER 1 TAKEAWAYS

Recognize and React: Identifying Stroke Symptoms

Understanding the signs of a stroke is crucial because time is of the essence. The faster you recognize the symptoms, the quicker you can get help, potentially preventing severe damage or even saving a life. Below is a checklist of the most common stroke symptoms. Take the time to memorize them and encourage others to do the same.

Encourage Others to Learn the Signs

While it's essential to know the signs of a stroke for your own safety, it's just as important to ensure that those around you—family, friends, coworkers—are also aware. Strokes often happen when we least expect them, and being prepared can save lives. Take a few minutes to talk to those close to you about the symptoms of a stroke Share the **FAST** acronym (**F**acial drooping, **A**rm weakness, **S**peech difficulties, **T**ime to call 911) as an easy way to remember the signs.

Stroke Symptom Checklist

- **Facial Drooping**: Is one side of the face drooping or numb? Ask the person to smile. Is their smile uneven?

- **Arm Weakness or Numbness**: Ask the person to raise both arms. Does one arm drift downward?

- **Speech Difficulties**: Is the person's speech slurred, or are they unable to speak or understand? Ask them to repeat a simple sentence like "The sky is blue."

- **Sudden Confusion**: Does the person suddenly seem confused, unable to think clearly, or understand what's happening around them?

- **Sudden Trouble Seeing**: Is there a sudden loss of vision or blurred vision in one or both eyes?

- **Sudden Trouble Walking**: Is there a loss of balance, coordination, or sudden dizziness?

- **Sudden Severe Headache**: Does the person experience a sudden, severe headache with no known cause?

    Remember: If you or someone else experiences any of these symptoms, act fast—call 911 immediately. Every second counts.

Start Conversations

Set a goal to talk to at least three people this week about the signs of a stroke. Explain why it's crucial to know these symptoms and how quick action can make all the difference.

·Share Resources: Distribute stroke symptom checklists or direct people to reliable online resources where they can learn more. Consider sharing your knowledge on social media to reach a broader audience.

Lead by Example

Encourage others to share this information with their own networks. The more people who know how to recognize a stroke, the safer our communities will be.

Recognizing stroke symptoms is a vital skill that can save lives, including your own. But it doesn't stop there. By sharing this knowledge with others, you can create a ripple effect that increases awareness and preparedness in your community. Strokes can happen to anyone, but together, we can ensure that more people are ready to respond quickly and effectively.

CHAPTER TWO
MAPPING THE TERRAIN
NAVIGATING RECOVERY

BIG JAKE'S STROKE OF GENIUS 24

MAPPING THE TERRAIN
NAVIGATING RECOVERY

May 12th, 2023, started like every other beautiful day on the island of Guam. There was a magnificent sunrise, and I had a great morning run. I was looking forward to having another great day of coaching the Guam high school Panthers as the head football coach. Despite the drama I was navigating through due to the inept school administration I, truly enjoyed coaching. On my way to practice, I had a wonderful conversation with the love of my life, Katrina Montez. As usual, I told her I looked forward to speaking with her again after practice. Upon arriving, I was immediately met with another stressful situation. (Note - Managing your stress is another key to stroke prevention. If it costs you your peace, it is too high of a price.) I saw the players on the field when they should have been in the locker room or in our film room staying cool before practice. During this time of the day in Guam, which is located only 5 degrees from the equator, the temperature usually hovers around 90 degrees with high humidity. Neither the players, my coaching staff nor I, were accustomed to being outside on the turf during this time. The heat is unbearable. I immediately confronted the school administrator who made the decision to put the players on the field without speaking to me first. I now realize that was not a good idea because the argument that occurred caused my blood pressure to spike.

Despite my protest, we attempted to have the players practice with modified gear to keep them cool and safe. About 20 minutes into practice, I could feel that it was a different level of heat and humidity. This was due to the tropical storm that was brewing to the south of

the island over the Pacific Ocean. I was demonstrating a play to our offense. The center snapped the ball to me, and in my mind, I caught it like I'd done countless times before. However, the ball went past me and landed at the feet of the coaches standing behind me. They immediately recognized that I had lost the feeling in my right hand and suspected that I was having a stroke. They started asking me to repeat simple sentences. When I could not respond they informed me that they were going to call the ambulance. At that point, I lost consciousness. I woke up in the hospital and was informed that I had brain surgery because of a stroke. I was not able to move the right side of my body. I immediately set a goal to walk out of the hospital. In the 1960's physical therapist, Signe Brunnstrom, developed a tool for charting a person's progress to stroke recovery that is still widely used today. The Brunnstrom stages describe the development of the ability to move and the reorganization of the brain after a stroke. This approach allows people who have had a stroke and their doctors to check the progress of their recovery. **The six stages are as follows:**
Stage 1: Flaccidity - During the first stage, a person is unable to move their muscles, and they may feel limp and floppy.
I remember feeling like a rag doll. All the muscles I prided myself on and spent time in the gym every day building were now useless.

Stage 2: Onset of spasticity - A person's muscles may now tighten involuntarily in response to a stimulus, such as a prod with a finger. However, the person may also have difficulty relaxing their muscles. This is the stage where I recall squeezing Katrina's hand tighter than usual. I was unable to relax my hand even when she asked me to. This led to my first bout of depression because I felt like I was hurting the person I claimed to love. She had flown 9,000 miles just to see me. I

like I'd run a marathon. I was tired, but I felt like I'd won a gold medal.

Stage 6: Spasticity disappears, and coordination returns - A person's control of their movements almost fully returns to typical function. Involuntary muscle tightening disappears, and the person's movements become more coordinated. Better every day! I continue to progress due to physical and mental health therapy. This is an ongoing stage for me.

> **While these stages provide a helpful roadmap for physical recovery, I've found that the journey also requires a strong mental and emotional foundation. Let's explore the keys that helped me navigate this terrain.**

These are the stages according to Brunnstrom, but from my personal experience I found that the primary key to your recovery is a **positive state of mind**. We can overcome the flaccid nature of stroke affected limbs. Yes, physical therapy is necessary, although it's common to feel like it's a waste of time during the early stages of recovery. Although it may feel like physical therapy is progressing slowly, it's important to recognize that each session builds the foundation for future recovery. Physical therapy is where the groundwork is laid—each repetition and exercise is a step toward regaining control. Pairing this physical work with a positive mindset accelerates progress and keeps you focused on the end goal. The dedicated men and women who serve as physical therapists are doing the grunt work that will eventually get us back on your feet and moving towards our goals. However, the key element is a positive mindset. I encourage you to develop a positive self-talk routine going into physical therapy.

My firsthand recovery experience has led me to the belief that we must first accept the fact that we've had a stroke. This can be a very challenging and daunting part of the recovery process, especially for someone who lived an active lifestyle. The mental aspect of coming to grips with not having the independence you once enjoyed can be overwhelming and give way to depression and suicidal ideology. I would highly suggest in this very first stage establishing a relationship with a mental health professional. The mental health component is just as important as physical therapy. I believe this is the reason why I have been able to do so well with my recoveries.

The second key to recovery is **acceptance**. I had to accept my new body and the physical limitations that were presented to me. This is where I encourage all stroke warriors to adopt a military mindset. In the military, we were trained to adapt quickly, think strategically, and persevere no matter the obstacles. During my recovery, this mindset became crucial. For example, when I was struggling to regain basic motor skills, I treated each small step moving forward—like lifting my arm—as a mission objective. I broke down my recovery into manageable tasks, just as I would approach a mission, focusing on one goal at a time and adjusting my strategy as needed. This approach kept me disciplined and motivated, helping me to maintain momentum even when progress was slow. In the military, we were trained to adjust fire and keep moving to win the war. This is where we must set SMART goals. (Specific, Measurable, Attainable, Realistic, Timely)

The third key to my recovery is **celebration**. I learned to celebrate even the small gains. This is important because the limbs that are affected are made up of a complex system of nerves and muscles that are connected and communicate seamlessly. When you have a stroke, the communication links between the nerves and muscles are disconnected. So, when you start to have small reconnections, you should celebrate each one like it's the Super bowl. This will ultimately lead to an atmosphere of celebration in your daily walk toward complete recovery. When I first managed to move my fingers, I celebrated by treating myself to my favorite dessert. Every small victory became a moment to share with my loved ones, creating an atmosphere of positivity and encouragement. These celebrations, no matter how small, kept me motivated and reminded me that each step forward was a significant achievement in my journey.

The fourth key to recovery is to **find your rhythm**. Brunnstrom speaks of regaining spasticity. Movement is the key now that you have more control over your limbs.

In this chapter, we focused on the stages of stroke recovery and learned about overcoming emotional and physical challenges. We also learned to set realistic recovery goals and understand the recovery process. Remember, nothing is easy about recovery. Give yourself some grace, find a support system and keep moving every day. If you had a stroke and you are reading this, you are a stroke SURVIVOR and not a victim. You are still here for a reason. Make the best out of every moment. No time wasted!

Recovery from a stroke is not just a physical journey; it's a mental and emotional one as well. By understanding the stages of recovery, adopting a positive mindset, setting SMART goals, celebrating each milestone, and staying in tune with your progress, you can navigate the terrain of recovery with determination and hope. Remember, each small step forward is a victory, and with the right mindset and support, you can overcome the challenges ahead.

CHAPTER 2 TAKEAWAYS

Creating Your Personal Recovery Guide: Reflecting on your current stage of recovery helps you understand where you are and what you've accomplished so far. It's important to acknowledge your physical and emotional state, as this will guide the next steps in your recovery process.

Step 1: Reflect on Your Current Stage
Based on the Brunnstrom stages of recovery, identify your current stage. Describe your physical and emotional state.

WHAT PHYSICAL ABILITIES HAVE YOU REGAINED?

THINK ABOUT HOW MUCH MOBILITY OR STRENGTH YOU'VE REGAINED, SUCH AS BEING ABLE TO MOVE A LIMB, STAND, OR WALK.

_____
_____
_____
_____
_____
_____
_____

WHAT ARE YOUR BIGGEST CHALLENGES?

CONSIDER ANY PHYSICAL OR EMOTIONAL CHALLENGES THAT ARE STILL AFFECTING YOU, LIKE MUSCLE WEAKNESS, FATIGUE, OR ANXIETY.

_____
_____
_____
_____
_____
_____
_____

HOW DO YOU FEEL ABOUT YOUR RECOVERY JOURNEY?

REFLECT ON YOUR EMOTIONAL STATE. ARE YOU HOPEFUL OR FRUSTRATED? BE HONEST WITH YOURSELF!

_____
_____
_____
_____
_____
_____
_____

Step 2: Set SMART Goals for Recovery

Setting SMART (Specific, Measurable, Achievable, Realistic, Time-based) goals allows you to create a clear plan for your recovery. These goals should be both realistic and motivating, giving you direction and focus as you move forward.

Use the SMART framework to set one or two goals for the next stage of your recovery.

WHAT SPECIFIC IMPROVEMENT ARE YOU AIMING FOR?

YOU MAY AIM TO WALK A SPECIFIC DISTANCE, IMPROVE YOUR SPEECH, OR REGAIN CONTROL OF A SPECIFIC MUSCLE GROUP.

_____
_____
_____
_____
_____
_____
_____
_____

HOW WILL YOU MEASURE YOUR PROGRESS?

THINK ABOUT HOW YOU WILL TRACK YOUR PROGRESS. FOR EXAMPLE, YOU MIGHT COUNT THE NUMBER OF STEPS YOU TAKE EACH DAY...

_____
_____
_____
_____
_____
_____
_____

WHAT TIMEFRAME WILL YOU SET TO ACHIEVE THIS GOAL?

CONSIDER HOW MUCH TIME IT WILL REALISTICALLY TAKE TO REACH THIS GOAL. MAKE SURE THE TIMEFRAME IS CHALLENGING BUT ATTAINABLE.

_____
_____
_____
_____
_____
_____
_____

Step 3: Develop Positive Self-Talk

Developing positive self-talk is a powerful tool in recovery. Your mindset influences your resilience, and the way you talk to yourself can determine your progress. Positive affirmations help you stay focused, motivated, and encouraged, especially on tough days.

Write down positive affirmations or phrases that encourage resilience and positivity during your recovery.

POSITIVE AFFIRMATIONS

"I AM STRONGER EVERY DAY," OR "I CAN OVERCOME THIS CHALLENGE." KEEP THEM SHORT, UPLIFTING, AND SPECIFIC TO YOUR RECOVERY.

_____

_____

_____

_____

_____

_____

_____

_____

POSITIVE AFFIRMATIONS CONTINUED

Step 4: Plan Your Celebrations

Celebrating progress is essential to staying motivated during recovery. It's easy to get caught up in focusing on what still needs to be done, but acknowledging your victories—no matter how small—keeps your spirits high and reinforces positive behaviors.

Plan how you will celebrate your next recovery milestone.

HOW WILL YOU REWARD YOURSELF?

THINK ABOUT WHAT WOULD FEEL LIKE A REWARD—MAYBE A SPECIAL TREAT, A DAY OUT, OR A MOMENT OF RELAXATION.

_____
_____
_____
_____
_____
_____
_____
_____
_____

HOW WILL YOU SHARE YOUR SUCCESS WITH OTHERS?

CONSIDER SHARING YOUR WIN WITH SOMEONE WHO HAS SUPPORTED YOU OR A COMMUNITY GROUP TO INSPIRE OTHERS.

BIG JAKE'S STROKE OF GENIUS   **38**

CHAPTER THREE

STRENGTHENING THE MIND

COGNITIVE AND EMOTIONAL HEALING

BIG JAKE'S STROKE OF GENIUS **40**

STRENGTHENING THE MIND
COGNITIVE AND EMOTIONAL HEALING

It was a beautiful Sunday morning in September. It was the perfect time to get a little exercise outside before the football games started. Katrina wanted to take a quick walk in the neighborhood. This would have been something that I would normally be game for pre-stroke. Running five miles was the norm on a day like this. However, I found myself inundated with thoughts of my limitations, both physical and mental. So, my goal was to make it to the dog park and back, which was approximately 200 yards, a five-minute walk. When we made it to the dog park, the most incredible thing happened. Katrina reached for my hand. Little did she know, I wanted to give up at that moment. But her small significant gesture of love energized me. I was able to continue the walk and use all my fine motor skills required to open the apartment building door, press the elevator button and use the key to unlock the door. These may seem like small tasks, but mental fortitude is required to get them done. Like cooking and bathing, they have far reaching effects and are more complex everyday tasks. When you can accomplish them, you have a sense of independence and hope for full recovery. This experience taught me the importance of both mental and emotional strength in recovery, and it's something I've worked hard to cultivate ever since. Let's explore how emotional support and daily practices can strengthen your mind during recovery.

According to the American Stroke Association around 10% of people who have a stroke will have a complete recovery. With this statistic being so low, it is vital to remain hopeful and engage in daily positive self-talk. It's even more important to have a strong mindset to achieve a successful recovery. The emotional component of recovery is highly dependent upon your support system. During my strokes, I was fortunate enough to have been in a relationship with Katrina. She was and continues to be very supportive and understanding of the recovery process. This is especially important because of the plethora of medications we, as stroke survivors, are often prescribed. These medications alter our mood and emotional state of mind. Having Katrina by my side gave me the emotional strength to push through difficult days. Whether it was a simple gesture like holding my hand or encouraging me to keep going, her support was invaluable. For those without a partner, I encourage finding support through family, friends, or stroke support groups, which can provide the encouragement and understanding you need. I highly suggest stroke survivors and caregivers utilize the Stroke Family Warmline. It is a free service that connects stroke survivors, their families, and caregivers with a team member who can provide support information and a listening ear. Many team members on the warmline are stroke survivors themselves or have a family member who are. My personal experience with the stroke support group has been amazing. I look forward to becoming a stroke recovery ambassador at my local hospital.

There are several other techniques I use to cope with my recovery process that specifically helps with strengthening my mind:

> **Daily Affirmations**: I employ the power of "yet". For example, "I may not be able to walk the entire block "yet", but I am getting better every day."

Meditation/Prayer: Daily meditation and prayer helps me feel more relaxed and calmer when anxiety, anger or fear begins to creep in.

Exercise/Dancing (even if it's seated): The music creates a sense of joy and happiness. The movement of dancing gives a sense of freedom and independence.

Go outside/sunlight: There are many benefits of sunlight to include lowering blood pressure, uplifting your mood and increasing your energy.

Eating healthy (fresh fruits and vegetables): Consuming vegetables and fruits can also lower your blood pressure as well as reduce the risk of heart disease and stroke.

These are just some of the techniques that I have implemented on my road to recovery. I encourage you to be intentional about creating new healthy habits that put you on the road to 120/80. I am confident that you can do it. We are in this together. We can strengthen our mental resilience and cognitive function through practical exercises such as memory games and puzzles.

Cognitive and emotional healing are just as vital as physical recovery after a stroke. By embracing support, engaging in positive self-talk, and implementing daily practices that nurture your mind and spirit, you can build the resilience needed to face each day with strength and hope. Remember, every small step forward is a victory, and together, we can navigate this journey toward recovery.

Chapter 3 Takeaways

Strengthening Your Mind with Cognitive Challenges

Engaging in cognitive exercises daily is crucial for improving mental clarity, memory, and overall brain function during recovery. Cognitive challenges not only stimulate your brain but also help in strengthening your resilience and maintaining mental wellness. Below are three simple activities to help you build a sharper, more focused mind, along with additional ways to support each exercise.

Crossword Puzzles and Sudoku

These puzzles are effective in boosting problem-solving skills, memory retention, and cognitive agility.

- **Activity**: Dedicate 10-15 minutes daily to solve a crossword puzzle or a Sudoku.
- **Additional Idea**: Puzzle Apps – Download puzzle apps that challenge your cognitive abilities and offer daily puzzles at varying levels. This can be an easy way to engage your brain on the go.
- **Challenge**: Track your progress and aim to improve your time or accuracy. Set a weekly goal to complete a puzzle in less time or solve a more difficult puzzle.

Memory Games

Memory exercises help to improve recall, attention, and focus. Whether it's a card matching game or a digital memory app, consistent practice can make a significant difference.

- **Activity**: Start with simple matching games, gradually increasing difficulty as you progress.
- **Additional Idea**: Memory Jar – Write down a list of items (e.g., fruits, animals, or random words) on pieces of paper. Read through the list once, then try to remember and write down as many items as you can after a short time.
- **Challenge**: Try using new memory tools such as apps designed to improve your memory or create a flashcard deck to review new words, facts, or concepts daily.

Learning New Skills or Information

Learning something new each day can stimulate your brain and enhance neuroplasticity. This can be as simple as learning a new word, trying a new recipe, or watching an educational video.

- **Activity**: Dedicate 10-15 minutes each day to learning a new skill or piece of information.
- **Additional Idea**: Skill-Based Learning – Try a simple online tutorial or craft project that involves problem-solving, such as learning to draw, knitting, or mastering a new cooking technique.
- **Challenge**: Create a learning journal to track new skills or knowledge. At the end of each week, reflect on your progress and add a new challenge for the following week, such as learning a more advanced skill.

WORD SEARCH

```
P G N S N S R G L O V G
A R T Y U U E N S N E V
F R I M V P S R R C T N
A E T P A P N C T E E I
S S S T R O K E E I Y I
T I N O I R O P U T C L
Y L T M L T T R S R I E
I I T S P P B R V R T R
R E C O V E R Y I T P Y
O N N U S S A E L I I T
G C H E A L I N G A T E
H E E C O G N I T I V E
```

STROKE	BRAIN	HEALING	FAST
RECOVERY	SYMPTOMS	SUPPORT	RECOVERY
AFFIRMATIONS	COGNITIVE	REHABILITATION	GOALS

BIG JAKE'S STROKE OF GENIUS

CHAPTER FOUR

THE SUPPORT SQUAD
BUILDING A STRONG NETWORK

BIG JAKE'S STROKE OF GENIUS 48

THE SUPPORT SQUAD
BUILDING A STRONG NETWORK

When I woke up in the hospital bed in Guam, I immediately realized something was different. I could not see out of my left eye, and I could not move the right side of my body. When I looked around the room, sitting to the right side of me was coach Kevin Manns, my assistant coach and someone who had grown to be my best friend and confidant. On Guam, he was the only other person I knew who had hauled pulpwood like I did when I was a kid. We nick-named each other "Pulpwood Hauler". Once coach Manns saw that I was awake and responsive, he informed me that I suffered a stroke. He said he already contacted "sis" (Katrina) who was in Texas at the time. He also told me he contacted Dr. Bailey, one of my closest friends, who worked in Korea. He started telling me about all the people who wanted to come to see me. This made me realize the importance of the relationships I had built during my 18 years living and working on Guam. I had no blood family there, but I had built the most amazing network of friends who became family. Every day I was in the hospital I had visitors. They were either there virtually or physically there at the hospital. To my surprise, my youngest sister made the 9,000-mile trip to come be by my side as well. Shortly after, Katrina arrived. I was overjoyed to see her, but I did not know how she would accept me as half a person. When we locked eyes, her smile reassured me that although I could not feel half of my body, she loved the whole of me. A week after Katrina's arrival, the island was hit by a category five typhoon. Katrina stayed by my side the entire time. She was there to assist the nurses and all the hospital staff with taking care of me, including helping with changing my adult diaper. One of my physical therapists in the hospital just happened to be one of my former football players. This was an example of the importance of pouring into people and reaping your harvest. He was once someone I coached, mentored and served as a role model to and now he was there taking care of me. He reminded me of some of the things I had said and done for him. I recall him saying, "Coach, you didn't let me give up. I'm not going to let you give up."

After being in the hospital for two weeks, I was finally cleared to go home. Katrina was still there by my side, but she would have to leave soon due to her military obligation. She knew I would need help so prior to her leaving she assembled "Team Jacob". This was my island family that consisted of coworkers from Andersen elementary school where I worked for 18 years, coaches, football players, neighbors, church members and my adopted daughter, Brooklynn, who was the leader of the operation. These amazing people were there helping me around the clock. They made sure I had breakfast, lunch and dinner. They showed up to give me my medication on time and kept a running log. They made sure a took showers daily. They took me to my doctor's appointments and to run other errands. My other adopted daughter, Kaylin Mills, would come by and sing to me to keep me in good spirits. When I decided to leave the island, a team was assembled to help with the moving process as well. My friend of 24 years, Angela Hampton, even volunteered to fly from Guam to Jacksonville, Florida with me.

As I continue my recovery, my network of supporters remains highly important to me. I was even fortunate enough to reconnect with my best friend since pre-K, Gerald Bryant. He and his wife, Andrea aka

"Best", have been a crucial part of my recovery success thus far. Everyone who stepped in to help me has played a vital role in my life. If it had not been for them, I would not have made it this far. I stayed with several relatives and friends for short periods of time throughout this journey. I am grateful for them all.

You may not have a large support system like I had during the early stages of my recovery but work with what you have. I now utilize face-to-face support groups in the community and social media resources for support. I encourage you to do the same. According to stroke.org, many survivors experience meaningful value from peer support. Research shows that peer support groups play an important role on stroke recovery by providing tools for effective coping, alleviating psychological stress, and creating an outlet for stroke survivors and caregivers. Take time to think about your team of supporters and let them know how much you appreciate them.

CHAPTER 4 TAKEAWAYS

Building Your Support Squad

The strength of your recovery depends heavily on the strength of your support network. In this chapter, we'll explore how a diverse group of supporters can play a vital role in stroke recovery. Whether it's family, friends, coworkers, or mentors, every person who offers help, encouragement, and love contributes to your healing journey. You don't need a large network—start with what you have and build from there. The key is recognizing the value of your relationships and showing gratitude for the people who are in your corner. Let's dive into an activity to help you map and strengthen your support system.

Activity: Building Your Support Squad

Start by identifying your support network—those who have been there for you or who you know will be there as you continue your recovery journey. This could be family, friends, healthcare professionals, or even community members.

LIST YOUR CURRENT SUPPORT SYSTEM

WHO ARE THE PEOPLE YOU CAN COUNT ON DURING YOUR RECOVERY?

_____ _____

_____ _____

_____ _____

_____ _____

_____

IDENTIFY AREAS OF SUPPORT

WHAT KIND OF HELP DO YOU NEED? IS IT EMOTIONAL, PHYSICAL, OR LOGISTICAL?

_____

_____

_____

_____

Reach out: Contact at least one person from your support network today to express gratitude and strengthen your relationship.

CHAPTER FIVE

A NEW MISSION
LIVING BEYOND RECOVERY

BIG JAKE'S STROKE OF GENIUS 54

A NEW MISSION

LIVING BEYOND RECOVERY

As a result of having multiple strokes, I started having seizures. I had survived the most violent seizure I ever experienced thus far. I was on Guam at the time. I recall hearing the long-sustained beeping sound that indicated I had flatlined. In the past, I've heard that your hearing is the last sense to go when transitioning. But in true warrior fashion, that was not the end of my story. After having many tests run, my neurologist informed me that she and her team had diagnosed me with Epilepsy. My knowledge of Epilepsy was very limited. My only experience with it was watching the chaos and panic of my neighbor and friend, Willie Williamson. His son had an Epileptic seizure years ago. The ambulance was called, and little Joshua was taken to the hospital. He was only about seven years old at the time. My neurologist told me that kids were often impacted by Epilepsy. I learned that Epilepsy is a seizure disorder in which nerve cell activity in the brain is disturbed. Epilepsy may occur because of a genetic disorder or an acquired brain injury, such as trauma or stroke. With this newfound knowledge, I knew that I had to become an Epilepsy warrior. This was not just my fight. According to the Epilepsy Foundation, approximately 1 in 26 people will develop Epilepsy at some point in their lives, highlighting the importance of awareness and support for those affected by this condition.

With the support of the love of my life, Katrina, we created "Love Always Wins" apparel to bring awareness and financial support to the fight against Epilepsy. Shortly after creating the apparel, "THE Love Always Wins Podcast" was created. The mission of "THE Love Always

Wins Podcast" is to encourage, inspire and empower the listeners to focus on the opportunities in life and not the obstacles. Katrina and I share our personal stories and life lessons and invite special guests to share their personal stories and life lessons as well. We recently had the opportunity to share the story of a perfectly fit bodybuilder who is over 50 years old, Jennifer. One day she was in the gym proudly posting her progress on social media. In less the 24 hours later, she was in the hospital. Unfortunately, she fell out of bed while having a seizure and hit her head on her nightstand. The blow to her head damaged the nerves connected to her legs. She now must learn how to walk again. After speaking with her, she informed us that she was diagnosed with Epilepsy at a young age. Prior to this happening, she hadn't had an episode in over eight years. We shared Jennifer's story on our podcast and provided our listeners with knowledge about Epileptic seizures and how they could provide support. We were able to bless Jennifer with much needed financial support during her recovery. This is just the beginning of my new mission and purpose in life. I've always had a passion to help people, especially children. Now I can continue to help, but in a different way.

I encourage you to write down things that make you feel the most energized about life. Analyze your list and decide on what you can pour your energy into post-recovery. Find your own mission, whether through advocacy, community work, or personal growth. How can you turn your experience into an opportunity to help others? What do you envision and plan for a fulfilling life post-recovery? Adapt to this new life. No! Things are not the same. Yes! We miss our old pre stroke lives, but I submit that our stroke experience and the fact that we are survivors uniquely qualifies us to speak life into people who may be experiencing other life challenges. We are still here for a reason. Let's play the cards we were dealt and get the victory in the end.

While my new mission became clear through our work with 'Love Always Wins,' I also knew that taking care of my physical health would be key to maintaining my energy and focus on this mission. That's why I developed a fitness routine to stay strong and energized for the long-term. I base my fitness routine on my favorite number, five. I do five sets of five reps with light weights and five minutes of rest with hydration between each set. You can also do this without using weights and tailor it to your own fitness level or ability. In the military, when we were deployed and did not have access to the gym or weights, we would use our own body resistance. For example, take your right hand and grasp your left wrist. Then do a curling motion with your left arm to curl your bicep. Create tension by pressing your right hand down as much as possible while you are curling your left arm. This is also a secondary tri-cep workout for your right arm. Another simple but effective movement I have found to be beneficial at every stage of my recovery is the "sit to stand" exercise. While safely seated at the edge of the chair and your feet flat on the floor, slowly stand. If needed, use the arms of the chair or a sturdy secure object to assist you with standing. Over time, the goal is to sit and stand without the assistance of an object. I end my fitness routine with a 15-minute walk, preferably outside. Again, tailor this to your own fitness level and ability. Use the "The 21-day Wellness Journey" at the end of the book to help guide you to a healthier lifestyle and successful recovery.

I am intentional about living a plant-based lifestyle as much as possible which has been proven to have many benefits. My recent blood work results showed little to no inflammation in my body. My doctor attributes this to my plant-based eating habit. I also feel lighter and more energetic due to the increase of more fresh fruits and veggies. I highly recommend adopting a habit of having your meal consisting of 75% veggies and fresh fruit, like the "Blue Zone" lifestyle. The Blue Zone lifestyle is a way of living that is associated with geographic areas where people tend to live longer and healthier lives. The Blue Zone diet is an eating pattern that focuses on plant-based foods and limits meat, dairy, eggs and sugar. Other common lifestyle features include moving naturally, finding the right tribe, having a positive life outlook and eating wisely.

Statistics on long-term health outcomes and quality of life for stroke survivors vary depending on age and the severity of the stroke. However, the American Stroke Association provide daily living recovery tips for all stroke survivors. I encourage you to view the tips on bathing, dressing, driving and shopping on stroke.org. Also, continue to attend physical and occupational therapy and take advantage of the expertise of mental health professionals regularly. This will help you stay motivated and maintain health and wellness long-term. Physical therapy has been extremely important to me. It has helped me regain mobility and freed me from the walker and wheelchair which were my two main goals when I started physical therapy. Mental health therapy plays a crucial role in total recovery. It has helped me with my depression and anxiety that was brought on because of my strokes. Now is the time to act. Whether it's developing a new fitness routine, advocating for a cause you care about, or finding new ways to live with purpose, you have the power to shape your future. You are a survivor, and the world needs your strength.

Chapter 5 Takeaways

Creating Your New Mission

1. **Reflect on Your Journey**, take a moment to reflect on your personal recovery journey so far. Write down what you've learned, the obstacles you've overcome, and the strengths you've discovered within yourself.

REFLECT ON YOUR JOURNEY

WHAT HAS RECOVERY TAUGHT YOU ABOUT YOURSELF?

_____
_____
_____
_____
_____
_____
_____
_____
_____
_____
_____

REFLECT ON YOUR JOURNEY

HOW HAVE YOU GROWN OR CHANGED THROUGH THE CHALLENGES YOU'VE FACED?

2. Define Your New Mission, based on your reflections, think about a new mission or cause you'd like to dedicate yourself to, whether it's personal or something that benefits others. This could be a cause related to your recovery, such as advocating for stroke awareness or supporting others facing similar challenges.

DEFINE YOUR NEW MISSION

WHAT CAUSE / MISSION EXCITES YOU AND FEELS ALIGNED WITH YOUR NEW PURPOSE IN LIFE?

_____

_____

_____

_____

_____

_____

_____

_____

_____

_____

DEFINE YOUR NEW MISSION

HOW CAN YOU TAKE SMALL STEPS TOWARD MAKING THIS MISSION A REALITY?

3. Set Actionable Goals for Your Mission

Create specific, measurable goals that will help you take tangible steps toward fulfilling your new mission.

YOUR MISSION GOALS

WHAT IS ONE SMALL, ACHIEVABLE GOAL YOU CAN SET TODAY TO START WORKING ON YOUR MISSION?

_____

_____

_____

_____

_____

_____

_____

_____

_____

_____

_____

_____

_____

YOUR MISSION GOALS

HOW WILL YOU TRACK YOUR PROGRESS AND CELEBRATE THE MILESTONES ALONG THE WAY?

4. Identify Resources and Support

Identify any resources, support systems, or individuals who can help you achieve your mission. This could include friends, family, professionals, or community organizations.

RESOURCES AND SUPPORT

WHO CAN SUPPORT YOU IN YOUR MISSION?

_____

_____

_____

_____

_____

_____

_____

_____

_____

_____

4. Identify Resources and Support

Identify any resources, support systems, or individuals who can help you achieve your mission. This could include friends, family, professionals, or community organizations.

RESOURCES AND SUPPORT

WHAT RESOURCES WILL HELP YOU MOVE FORWARD?

_____
_____
_____
_____
_____
_____
_____
_____
_____
_____

21 DAY
WELLNESS JOURNEY

As you embark on this journey, it's essential to assess where you currently stand in your recovery process. This assessment will help you reflect on your support systems, coping mechanisms, and readiness to engage in the transformative work that lies ahead.

NOTES AND REFLECTION
Transforming Your Stroke Recovery into a Journey of Strength and Hope

_____
_____
_____
_____
_____
_____
_____
_____
_____
_____
_____
_____
_____
_____
_____
_____
_____
_____
_____
_____
_____
_____
_____
_____
_____
_____
_____

21-DAY WELLNESS JOURNEY
DAY 1

__ / __ / ____

RECOGNIZE STROKE SYMPTOMS

Morning

TIME	SYSTOLIC (UPPER)	DIASTOLIC (LOWER)	HEART RATE

Activity: Review the FAST (Face, Arms, Speech, Time) Share "FAST" with at least one person.

Evening

TIME	SYSTOLIC (UPPER)	DIASTOLIC (LOWER)	HEART RATE

Gratitude: Write down one thing you appreciate about your health today.

NOTES AND REFLECTION

Transforming Your Stroke Recovery into a Journey of Strength and Hope

_____
_____
_____
_____
_____
_____
_____
_____
_____
_____
_____
_____
_____
_____
_____
_____
_____
_____
_____
_____
_____
_____
_____
_____
_____
_____
_____

21-DAY WELLNESS JOURNEY
DAY 2

__ / __ / ____

SET A RECOVERY GOAL

Morning

TIME	SYSTOLIC (UPPER)	DIASTOLIC (LOWER)	HEART RATE

Activity: Identify one specific, measurable goal for your recovery (e.g., walking 200 yards).

Evening

TIME	SYSTOLIC (UPPER)	DIASTOLIC (LOWER)	HEART RATE

Gratitude: Write down one thing you appreciate about your health today.

NOTES AND REFLECTION
Transforming Your Stroke Recovery into a Journey of Strength and Hope

_____
_____
_____
_____
_____
_____
_____
_____
_____
_____
_____
_____
_____
_____
_____
_____
_____
_____
_____
_____
_____
_____
_____
_____
_____

21-DAY WELLNESS JOURNEY
DAY 3

__ / __ / ____

COGNITIVE EXERCISE

Morning

TIME	SYSTOLIC (UPPER)	DIASTOLIC (LOWER)	HEART RATE

Activity: Spend 15 minutes on a cognitive puzzle or game (e.g., crossword, Sudoku).

Evening

TIME	SYSTOLIC (UPPER)	DIASTOLIC (LOWER)	HEART RATE

Gratitude: Note three small wins from your day.

NOTES AND REFLECTION
Transforming Your Stroke Recovery into a Journey of Strength and Hope

21-DAY WELLNESS JOURNEY
DAY 4

__ / __ / ____

REACH OUT TO YOUR SUPPORT SQUAD

Morning

TIME	SYSTOLIC (UPPER)	DIASTOLIC (LOWER)	HEART RATE

Activity: Contact a friend or family member to discuss your recovery journey and share updates.

Evening

TIME	SYSTOLIC (UPPER)	DIASTOLIC (LOWER)	HEART RATE

Gratitude: Write a thank-you note to someone who has supported you.

NOTES AND REFLECTION
Transforming Your Stroke Recovery into a Journey of Strength and Hope

_____
_____
_____
_____
_____
_____
_____
_____
_____
_____
_____
_____
_____
_____
_____
_____
_____
_____
_____
_____
_____
_____
_____
_____
_____

21-DAY WELLNESS JOURNEY
DAY 5

__ / __ / ____

CREATE YOUR NEW MISSION

Morning

TIME	SYSTOLIC (UPPER)	DIASTOLIC (LOWER)	HEART RATE

Activity: Write a short paragraph about a cause or mission you want to pursue post-recovery.

Evening

TIME	SYSTOLIC (UPPER)	DIASTOLIC (LOWER)	HEART RATE

Gratitude: Reflect on what you have learned through your challenges.

NOTES AND REFLECTION
Transforming Your Stroke Recovery into a Journey of Strength and Hope

_____
_____
_____
_____
_____
_____
_____
_____
_____
_____
_____
_____
_____
_____
_____
_____
_____
_____
_____
_____
_____
_____
_____
_____
_____
_____
_____

21-DAY WELLNESS JOURNEY
DAY 6

__ / __ / ____

EDUCATE YOURSELF

Morning

TIME	SYSTOLIC (UPPER)	DIASTOLIC (LOWER)	HEART RATE

Activity: Research one statistic about stroke recovery and share it on social media or with friends.

Evening

TIME	SYSTOLIC (UPPER)	DIASTOLIC (LOWER)	HEART RATE

Gratitude: List three aspects of your life you are thankful for today.

NOTES AND REFLECTION

Transforming Your Stroke Recovery into a Journey of Strength and Hope

_____
_____
_____
_____
_____
_____
_____
_____
_____
_____
_____
_____
_____
_____
_____
_____
_____
_____
_____
_____
_____
_____
_____
_____
_____
_____

21-DAY WELLNESS JOURNEY
DAY 7

__ / __ / ____

EVALUATE YOUR PROGRESS

Morning

TIME	SYSTOLIC (UPPER)	DIASTOLIC (LOWER)	HEART RATE

Activity: Write down your recovery goals and assess your progress toward them.

Evening

TIME	SYSTOLIC (UPPER)	DIASTOLIC (LOWER)	HEART RATE

Gratitude: Celebrate a win from the past week, big or small.

NOTES AND REFLECTION

Transforming Your Stroke Recovery into a Journey of Strength and Hope

21-DAY WELLNESS JOURNEY
DAY 8

__ / __ / ____

PRACTICE MINDFULNESS

Morning

TIME	SYSTOLIC (UPPER)	DIASTOLIC (LOWER)	HEART RATE

Activity: Spend 10 minutes practicing mindfulness or meditation.

Evening

TIME	SYSTOLIC (UPPER)	DIASTOLIC (LOWER)	HEART RATE

Gratitude: Journal about a positive experience from the past week.

NOTES AND REFLECTION
Transforming Your Stroke Recovery into a Journey of Strength and Hope

_____
_____
_____
_____
_____
_____
_____
_____
_____
_____
_____
_____
_____
_____
_____
_____
_____
_____
_____
_____
_____
_____
_____
_____
_____
_____
_____

21-DAY WELLNESS JOURNEY
DAY 9

___ / ___ / _____

JOIN A SUPPORT GROUP

Morning

TIME	SYSTOLIC (UPPER)	DIASTOLIC (LOWER)	HEART RATE

Activity: Research and join a local or online stroke support group.

Evening

TIME	SYSTOLIC (UPPER)	DIASTOLIC (LOWER)	HEART RATE

Gratitude: Thank someone who inspires you within your support network.

NOTES AND REFLECTION
Transforming Your Stroke Recovery into a Journey of Strength and Hope

_____
_____
_____
_____
_____
_____
_____
_____
_____
_____
_____
_____
_____
_____
_____
_____
_____
_____
_____
_____
_____
_____
_____
_____
_____

21-DAY WELLNESS JOURNEY
DAY 10
__ / __ / ____

VOLUNTEER OR ADVOCATE

Morning

TIME	SYSTOLIC (UPPER)	DIASTOLIC (LOWER)	HEART RATE

Activity: Find an organization related to stroke awareness and commit to volunteering or advocacy.

Evening

TIME	SYSTOLIC (UPPER)	DIASTOLIC (LOWER)	HEART RATE

Gratitude: Reflect on how you can make a difference in someone else's life.

NOTES AND REFLECTION
Transforming Your Stroke Recovery into a Journey of Strength and Hope

21-DAY WELLNESS JOURNEY
DAY 11

__ / __ / ____

ASSESS RISK FACTORS

Morning

TIME	SYSTOLIC (UPPER)	DIASTOLIC (LOWER)	HEART RATE

Activity: List your personal health habits and identify any potential risk factors for strokes.

Evening

TIME	SYSTOLIC (UPPER)	DIASTOLIC (LOWER)	HEART RATE

Gratitude: Write about a healthy habit you are proud of.

NOTES AND REFLECTION

Transforming Your Stroke Recovery into a Journey of Strength and Hope

21-DAY WELLNESS JOURNEY
DAY 12

__ / __ / ____

CREATE A DAILY ROUTINE

Morning

TIME	SYSTOLIC (UPPER)	DIASTOLIC (LOWER)	HEART RATE

Activity: Establish a daily routine that incorporates physical activity, nutrition, and rest.

Evening

TIME	SYSTOLIC (UPPER)	DIASTOLIC (LOWER)	HEART RATE

Gratitude: Acknowledge a small change you made in your routine that positively affected you.

NOTES AND REFLECTION
Transforming Your Stroke Recovery into a Journey of Strength and Hope

_____
_____
_____
_____
_____
_____
_____
_____
_____
_____
_____
_____
_____
_____
_____
_____
_____
_____
_____
_____
_____
_____
_____
_____

21-DAY WELLNESS JOURNEY
DAY 13

__ / __ / ____

CONNECT WITH A LOVED ONE

Morning

TIME	SYSTOLIC (UPPER)	DIASTOLIC (LOWER)	HEART RATE

Activity: Share your feelings and thoughts about your recovery with a loved one.

Evening

TIME	SYSTOLIC (UPPER)	DIASTOLIC (LOWER)	HEART RATE

Gratitude: List three things you are grateful for in your relationship with them.

NOTES AND REFLECTION

Transforming Your Stroke Recovery into a Journey of Strength and Hope

_____
_____
_____
_____
_____
_____
_____
_____
_____
_____
_____
_____
_____
_____
_____
_____
_____
_____
_____
_____
_____
_____
_____
_____
_____
_____
_____
_____
_____
_____

21-DAY WELLNESS JOURNEY
DAY 14

__ / __ / ____

PLAN A SOCIAL ACTIVITY

Morning

TIME	SYSTOLIC (UPPER)	DIASTOLIC (LOWER)	HEART RATE

Activity: Schedule a social outing (even virtually) with friends or family.

Evening

TIME	SYSTOLIC (UPPER)	DIASTOLIC (LOWER)	HEART RATE

Gratitude: Celebrate the connections you have with your support squad.

NOTES AND REFLECTION
Transforming Your Stroke Recovery into a Journey of Strength and Hope

_____
_____
_____
_____
_____
_____
_____
_____
_____
_____
_____
_____
_____
_____
_____
_____
_____
_____
_____
_____
_____
_____
_____
_____
_____
_____

21-DAY WELLNESS JOURNEY
DAY 15

__ / __ / ____

REFLECT ON YOUR JOURNEY

Morning

TIME	SYSTOLIC (UPPER)	DIASTOLIC (LOWER)	HEART RATE

Activity: Write a letter to your future self about your recovery goals and aspirations.

Evening

TIME	SYSTOLIC (UPPER)	DIASTOLIC (LOWER)	HEART RATE

Gratitude: Identify a lesson you learned through your experiences.

NOTES AND REFLECTION
Transforming Your Stroke Recovery into a Journey of Strength and Hope

21-DAY WELLNESS JOURNEY
DAY 16

__ / __ / ____

SHARE YOUR KNOWLEDGE

Morning

TIME	SYSTOLIC (UPPER)	DIASTOLIC (LOWER)	HEART RATE

Activity: Teach someone about stroke symptoms and prevention.

Evening

TIME	SYSTOLIC (UPPER)	DIASTOLIC (LOWER)	HEART RATE

Gratitude: Reflect on how sharing knowledge empowers you.

NOTES AND REFLECTION
Transforming Your Stroke Recovery into a Journey of Strength and Hope

21-DAY WELLNESS JOURNEY
DAY 17

__ / __ / ____

CELEBRATE PROGRESS

Morning

TIME	SYSTOLIC (UPPER)	DIASTOLIC (LOWER)	HEART RATE

Activity: Create a visual chart of your recovery goals and progress.

Evening

TIME	SYSTOLIC (UPPER)	DIASTOLIC (LOWER)	HEART RATE

Gratitude: Celebrate a specific milestone you've reached.

NOTES AND REFLECTION
Transforming Your Stroke Recovery into a Journey of Strength and Hope

_____
_____
_____
_____
_____
_____
_____
_____
_____
_____
_____
_____
_____
_____
_____
_____
_____
_____
_____
_____
_____
_____
_____
_____
_____
_____
_____

21-DAY WELLNESS JOURNEY
DAY 18

__ / __ / ____

ENGAGE IN A CREATIVE ACTIVITY

Morning

TIME	SYSTOLIC (UPPER)	DIASTOLIC (LOWER)	HEART RATE

Activity: Try a creative outlet (drawing, writing, music) to express your feelings.

Evening

TIME	SYSTOLIC (UPPER)	DIASTOLIC (LOWER)	HEART RATE

Gratitude: Acknowledge the creative process as part of your healing.

NOTES AND REFLECTION

Transforming Your Stroke Recovery into a Journey of Strength and Hope

21-DAY WELLNESS JOURNEY
DAY 19

__ / __ / ____

HOST A GRATITUDE GATHERING

Morning

TIME	SYSTOLIC (UPPER)	DIASTOLIC (LOWER)	HEART RATE

Activity: Organize a small gathering (in-person or virtual) to express gratitude to your support system.

Evening

TIME	SYSTOLIC (UPPER)	DIASTOLIC (LOWER)	HEART RATE

Gratitude: Share what you appreciate most about each person attending.

NOTES AND REFLECTION

Transforming Your Stroke Recovery into a Journey of Strength and Hope

21-DAY WELLNESS JOURNEY
DAY 20

__ / __ / ____

SET NEW GOALS

Morning

TIME	SYSTOLIC (UPPER)	DIASTOLIC (LOWER)	HEART RATE

Activity: Reflect on your journey and set new recovery goals for the next month.

Evening

TIME	SYSTOLIC (UPPER)	DIASTOLIC (LOWER)	HEART RATE

Gratitude: Celebrate the growth and change you've experienced.

NOTES AND REFLECTION
Transforming Your Stroke Recovery into a Journey of Strength and Hope

_____
_____
_____
_____
_____
_____
_____
_____
_____
_____
_____
_____
_____
_____
_____
_____
_____
_____
_____
_____
_____
_____
_____
_____

21-DAY WELLNESS JOURNEY
DAY 21   __ / __ / ____

REFLECTION AND CELEBRATION

Morning

TIME	SYSTOLIC (UPPER)	DIASTOLIC (LOWER)	HEART RATE

Activity: Review your 21-day journey. Write down what you learned and how you've grown.

Evening

TIME	SYSTOLIC (UPPER)	DIASTOLIC (LOWER)	HEART RATE

Gratitude: Celebrate your commitment to recovery and acknowledge your achievements.

NOTES AND REFLECTION

Transforming Your Stroke Recovery into a Journey of Strength and Hope

_____
_____
_____
_____
_____
_____
_____
_____
_____
_____
_____
_____
_____
_____
_____
_____
_____
_____
_____
_____
_____
_____
_____
_____
_____
_____
_____
_____
_____

BLOOD PRESSURE TRACKER

DATE	TIME	SYSTOLIC	DIASTOLIC	HEART RATE	NOTES

NOTES AND REFLECTION
Transforming Your Stroke Recovery into a Journey of Strength and Hope

BLOOD PRESSURE TRACKER

DATE	TIME	SYSTOLIC	DIASTOLIC	HEART RATE	NOTES

NOTES AND REFLECTION
Transforming Your Stroke Recovery into a Journey of Strength and Hope

BLOOD PRESSURE TRACKER

DATE	TIME	SYSTOLIC	DIASTOLIC	HEART RATE	NOTES

www.ingramcontent.com/pod-product-compliance
Lightning Source LLC
Chambersburg PA
CBHW080445110426
42743CB00016B/3284